HOW TO

PARENT

A GENIUS

RAISING KIDS THAT ARE SMART, SUCCESSFUL, NICE AND HAPPY

PAT QUINN

How to Parent a Genius

Raising Kids That are Smart, Successful,
Nice, and Happy!

By Pat Quinn

ISBN: 978-1544655291

Copyright 2017

All rights reserved.

Table of Contents

ABOUT THIS BOOK

THIS BOOK WILL COVER FOUR big topics: How to help your children grow up to be Smart, Successful, Nice, and Happy! The topics will be covered in reverse order. The first part of the book will show you how to help your children in each of these four areas. The second part of the book will give you a list of activities you can do with your children to grow and develop them in each of these areas.

Happy

Every parent wants their children to grow up to be happy, but how does that happen? This book will show you the four areas your child needs to master to be happy throughout life.

The first area is control. Your child needs to be able to be in control and also needs to be good at NOT being in control.

The second area is competence. Your child needs to be confident and believe they are competent in their own abilities.

The third area is relationships. Your child needs to be able to form and maintain relationships with other people.

The fourth area is relevance. Your child needs to have a plan for their life so that everything they are doing now is relevant.

Nice

One of the hardest things to do in life is to be right, without hurting other people. In other words, having the right answers is not the hard part, being nice about having the right answers is much more difficult. This section of the book will show you the two concepts your child needs to know and understand to be nice: Edify and Abundance.

Successful

There are many people who are really smart, but not really successful in life. This section of the book will focus on the two most important skills that all successful people share: goal-setting and progress-tracking.

Smart

This section of the book is saved for last because it is the easiest of the four. Every person is smart in certain ways. You might be book-smart, street-smart, or relationship-smart. Knowing your strengths and leveraging them is key to becoming Smart, Successful, Nice, and Happy!

Activities

The second part of this book is dedicated to giving you activities you can do with your children to help them grow and develop in each of these four areas. You probably won't do ALL of these activities (there are a lot of them!), but everyone that you do will help your children grow toward becoming a genius!

Thanks for joining me on this journey! Let's get started!

INTRODUCTION

MY NAME IS PAT QUINN, and I've been helping parents and teachers raise children who are smart, successful, nice, and happy for over 20 years. I've studied families and children as they learn and grow and develop, and I know what helps children grow into the productive, successful adults that we want them to be. The title of this book, *How to Parent a Genius*, may leave you wondering, *Is my child a genius?* Well, I will tell you this—I believe every child is a genius in one way or another. Your child may be super off-the-charts smart, or your child may be great at forming friendships and having great relationships. You child may be a great problem solver who is going to overcome any obstacle in their life, or your child may just know how to be happy and have fun in every situation.

Any of these are characteristics of a genius. If you think, *Well, my child's not smart enough to be a genius,* you need to broaden your perception of a genius. A genius is much more than someone who is just book smart. You might think, *Well, my child is little bit shy. They could never be a genius.* I assure you that every child is capable of being a genius. This book is designed to help every parent grow and develop their children into smart, successful, nice, and happy people. I know many children who are really smart. They get straight As in school. They score off-the-charts on those tests that kids take, but that doesn't mean that they're going to be successful, nice, or happy. I also know many children who are very successful. They do well in school. Maybe they do well in sports. They get scholarships. They appear from the outside to be very successful. That doesn't mean that other people view them as nice or as happy.

To be fully well rounded, to be fully developed, and to really have the life that we hope for our children, I believe we need our children to grow in all four of these areas: smart, successful, nice, and happy. This book is divided into sections, which are dedicated to each of these four areas. The book is actually organized in reverse order. I'm going to talk about happy first, because I believe if we can help our children be happy, they'll be much nicer people. I believe that when our children are nicer, they will be more successful. I believe that if you have a child who is happy, nice, and successful, that they are going to be much smarter, not only in school subjects and classes, but in life in general.

Each of the sections in this book will also include lists of activities that you can do with your children or talk to your children about to help develop this particular area in your child.

Thank you for your interest and willingness to take the time to help your child develop. I believe every child is a genius, and I know if you put the thought and effort into helping your child develop in these four areas, you will be doing everything you can to help raise your children to be smart, successful, nice, and happy.

PART 1:

THE FOUR FACTORS

SECTION 1:
HAPPY

TO RAISE CHILDREN WHO ARE "happy," you need to focus on four areas: control, competence, relationships, and relevance. Each of these four areas need to be modeled, taught, practiced, and monitored for growth. When you put the four areas together, your child has the very best chance of growing up to be happy!

Control

To become happy, your children need to understand control. Your child needs to be good at being in control ... and not being in control. It is the role of the parent to help your child when they are in situations where they can be in control, but also to help them when they are in situations where they are not in control. As your children develop, you need to help them in both situations.

Let's talk about being in control. To help our children understand what it means to be in control, we need to continually put them in situations where they're in control. This means giving them real decisions to make and honoring their decisions. This means giving them real problems to solve and listening to their solutions. This means asking them real questions and taking to heart their real answers.

When we go to our children and ask them for advice, ask them for suggestions, or ask them for solutions, we're putting them in control. If we ignore their answers, we teach them that they're never in control and being in control doesn't really matter; but when we take their answers, their suggestions, their solutions, and their advice seriously, we actually help them grow into positions of control. Now, like all good parenting, this is teaching. It is teaching your children how to not take advantage of the fact that they are in control, how to treat others fairly when they are in control, and how to be in control without having followers that hate them, but instead, to have followers who believe in and want to try to help them. There are many aspects to leadership and many aspects to being in control that don't come naturally to our children. If we have kids who are natural leaders, they might be very good at this and struggle when they have to give up control. We might have other children who struggle with being in control, but are very good followers. To really be happy, our children need to be good at both.

The other half of this is that sometimes you're not going to be in control. If you have a child who struggles with this, it's part of your role as a parent to help them become better followers and help them become better at giving up control to another person. As you go through day-to-day life, when you identify situations when you're not in control, you simply have to teach and talk your children through this process. When you get in a line and you can't make the line go any faster, talk about the fact that it's not really under your control—we just have to stand in this line. When you're choosing what game to play next, sometimes it's going to be your turn to choose the game, but other times, it's going to be someone else's turn to choose what you play next, and you need to give up that control.

There are ways to do this that make you a good follower. Do it without criticism, do it without complaining, and do it without negativity. Positively and enthusiastically support the decision that the other person made. There are many things we can teach our children that will help them become better followers, to become better at not being in control. Remember, to be truly happy, you have to be good when you're in control and when you're not in control. It's our job as parents to practice both of these situations, teach both of these situations, and certainly, to model both of these situations. If you're in a two-parent home, modeling the back and forth of control is one of the most valuable things you can do. You can model that sometimes you make the decisions and sometimes your spouse makes the decisions. For example: When my spouse makes the decisions, I'm supportive, I don't complain, I don't undercut. I can offer input, but I understand I'm not in control. This is all part of the process of developing children who can be both in control and not in control.

In this book, I have included a list of activities that you can do with your children that will help them learn how to be in control and practice it. These are not independent activities. The first time you do each of these activities, you should participate with your child and talk them through the activity, teaching them through the process of being in control. I've also included a list of activities you can do with your children that will help them learn how to not be in control. It's important to practice these, as well, so your children can be comfortable when they're not in control. You want to talk them through this process and teach them so they can become good followers when they're not in control. Make sure you do both sets of activities. Naturally, all children will be drawn more to one set of activities over the other set of activities. Most children either enjoy being in control or prefer not being in control and being a follower. It's your role as a parent to help develop both parts of their personality, both skillsets, so your child can be truly happy, whether or not they are in control.

Competence

Competence is the next skill that your child needs in order to be truly happy. Competence is the belief that you are doing okay. Competence is the belief that you are good enough. Competence is the belief in yourself that you are adequate and doing enough. All children struggle with the concept of competence at one point or another. Some students truly struggle in school, and they feel incompetent. Other students do very well in school, but still feel incompetent because they aren't perfect or aren't meeting high expectations. It is the role of parents to help children with the idea of competence and provide them with a set of activities and skills they can participate in and develop so they can truly be satisfied and feel competent.

As a parent, one of the first things we want to do is talk to our children about how they feel about themselves. One of my earliest conversations with my children were about their strengths and things they were good at. We play a game at my house called person of the moment.

Person of the moment is a game where one person at the table becomes the person of the moment. Then you go around the table and every other person sitting at the table will say one thing they like about the person of the moment. When it comes around to the person of the moment, they have to say something they like about themselves. Children love to play this game, because it allows them to say nice things about other people, but what it really does is it allows children to practice saying things they like about themselves. As soon as your children are old enough to talk, they should be able to tell you something they like about themselves, something that they're good at, one of their strengths. They should know good things about themselves that other people like. It's important that children have this positive view of themselves. Now that doesn't mean that they think they're above other people. It doesn't mean that they don't have any faults or never make mistakes, but more often than not, children will err on the other side of the spectrum and only see their mistakes, only see their weaknesses, only see their flaws, and won't be able to say anything good about themselves.

An honest and realistic view of their competence, adequacy, strengths, and what other people like about them is an important part of the child development process and an extremely important part of your child being happy throughout their lives. If you always rely on other people to make you happy, you're always going to be dependent upon praise and approval from other people. To truly live a happy life, it is better to develop in your children an accurate view of themselves, where they can be satisfied with how they are doing without the approval and praise of other people. If you develop this in your children, your children can be independently happy, regardless of the situation, without having to chase after other people's praise or seek other people's approval. To become true independent thinkers and sound decision makers, your children cannot be reliant on others for approval or praise.

When most children get in trouble for making bad decisions, giving into peer pressure, or participating in high-risk activities, this happens because they're seeking the approval of their peers and they believe if they don't do these obnoxious or dangerous things to achieve the approval of their peers, for some reason, they will not be worthy or not have any friends afterward. This is a sure sign that they have not fully developed their ability to be happy with just themselves, to be happy without the approval of others and without the praise of others. This concept of competence—the idea that I know my strengths, I know what I do well, I know that other people like me, I know that I'm good enough, I know that I'm adequate—is an extremely important part of the child development process if you want your children to be happy.

I have included a list of activities in this book that you can do with your children and things that you can say to your children that will help build their self-esteem, their competence, and an accurate and true view of their own competence that does not rely on other people's praise or approval.

Relationships

The next thing your children need to be happy is relationships. From the child's very earliest age, it is the role of a parent to teach, model, and practice healthy relationships. Your child might be a perfect student, score off the charts on every test, know every fact on the Internet, but if they don't have healthy relationships, people they can trust, share and laugh with, they are not going to be completely happy. Some children are extremely smart and bright; although they are very gifted in that skillset, they struggle in the interpersonal emotional intelligence relationship skillset. As parents, our job is to create a balanced set of skills in our children, where they are competent in relationship skills, just as they are in some of the academics or intelligence skills that we work so hard on.

What are the skills that a child needs to be happy in relationships? If you follow the process simply chronologically, the first set of skills would be about meeting new people and making new friends. How do you approach a group of people you don't yet know? How do you approach a person you don't know? How do you introduce yourself? How do you talk about yourself in a way that is intriguing, but not off putting? How do you immediately project that you are friendly and open to a new relationship? All of these things need to be taught, modeled, and practiced with your children. First of all, great parents talk about the importance of this and teach the skills that are necessary. Second, they model this in their own relationships. Then, after they model it for their children and in front of their children, they talk about and teach it. "Did you see what I did there? Did you see how I took advantage of that opportunity? Did you see any mistakes that I made? What could I have done differently to do even better next time?"

The one thing some parents do that others don't that makes a great difference is create opportunities to practice this. Of course, it's easier just to hang around with your good friends, but parents who are developing this skill in their children put them in situations where their children need to make new friends, so they don't always make the easiest decision, but instead, make the decision that will lead to a full and balanced development of their children. You want to look for opportunities to meet new people, pre-teach before you get into the situation, observe while your child is in the situation, and then debrief or post-teach after the situation. "What went well? What could have gone differently?" It's never too late to start teaching and practicing like this. If you have a child who is in their preteen or teenage years, or who is even in or already out of high school and is still struggling with this, you can still put them in situations where they can practice and improve.

Every time you practice it, it gets a little bit easier. Every time you pre-teach and post-teach, they get a little bit better. This may not be something that your children will ever be amazing at, it may not be their naturally gifted set of skills, but it is something that clearly can be developed and needs to be developed if you want your children to be completely happy.

After you get through the making of new friends, the next step is the maintenance of friendships. How do you maintain healthy friendships? What does that look like?

What activities do you participate in, and what activities do you avoid?

Once you've had these discussions and teachings with your children, the final set of skillsets you want to develop with your kids is conflict resolution. Every relationship, friendship, marriage, and parent-child relationship comes with conflict at some point.

Develop in your children a good set of conflict resolution skills, including ways to compromise, ways to talk to the other person without coming across as threatening or as a bully, ways to get their point across without being the one who always has to get their way, and as we've talked about previously, ways to be in control and to give up control. All of these are conflict resolution skills that will serve your children well as they grow and develop in relationships.

If you put these three together—making new friends, maintaining health relationships with friends, and working on conflict resolution when a relationship isn't going perfectly—you have the great foundation for a healthy relationship with your kids and you're helping your children build a foundation to have great relationships with others.

To help you and your child, I've included in this chapter a list of skills and things you can model, teach, and practice with them that will help them develop healthy relationship skills as they grow and develop.

Note: Just because this may not be your child's strength, it doesn't mean that you should ignore or avoid it. It's the parents who allow their children to avoid all relationship situations that wind up with kids who, although they may be really smart and maybe even really successful, may not be happy in life. Make sure you work on these skills as much as you do the academic and intelligence skills that your child may come to more easily.

Relevance

The fourth skill that your child needs in order to be happy is relevance. Relevance is the ability to attach all of the knowledge and learning they have received to a meaningful purpose in life. All of the facts and trivia they might know has no purpose or meaning if they don't have a way to attach it to their purpose in life.

Now, with really young children, it might seem a little silly to try to help them find their purpose in life or create a plan for the rest of their life. Here's what I know. I know that children are more motivated, learn better, and see a reason to develop all of their skillsets when they believe they are doing it in pursuit of a higher purpose. I also understand that a young child may not know what career they want for the rest of their lives. However, it's important to give them a goal that's greater than themselves. Children need to know that they're learning something for a reason—to help someone else, for a greater purpose, or for a goal that might be a month, six months, or six years away.

This is an important skill that every child needs to develop. Without the idea of relevance, students will become really book smart, but not very smart in life. They may get straight A's in school, but they won't do very well when real problems encounter them in real life. They understand how to fix an engine, but they've never actually fixed an engine. They understand how to do math, but they don't know how to use math outside of the textbook to solve real problems.

Attaching the knowledge, skills, and facts that they know to real-life situations and helping children develop a plan and goals for the rest of their life, or just for now, is an important part of helping your children develop into happy and productive adults. Help them understand that there is a bigger purpose to what they're learning. As they're absorbing the knowledge and skills they acquire and the things they observe, make sure you balance that with conversations about how they want to use all those skills. How do you want to use all of this knowledge? What's the greater purpose here? Sometimes, that will be short term, "In the next six months, we want to use these skills to do this; in the next year, we want to try to do this." Sometimes, it will be long term, "When you grow up, maybe you want to be a doctor; when you grow up, maybe you want to be an accountant."

Short term or long term, this gives a purpose or a context for all of the skills and knowledge your child is learning. Learning in context is always more meaningful, retained longer, and more motivating than learning without context. By helping your child attach everything they're learning to a purpose greater than themselves or to a plan for the rest of their lives, you are doing your child a great service and giving them a vital skill that will lead to true happiness.

I've included in this chapter a list of things you can do to help attach relevance to your child's learning. When these four elements, control, competence, relationships, and relevance, are combined, they are the foundation of helping your child become not just smart and successful, but also happy. If there is one true wish every parent has for their children, it is that they will be happy.

SECTION 2:
NICE

LET'S TALK ABOUT RAISING KIDS who are nice. Along with having children who are smart and successful, we also want them to be nice. I know so many children who are really smart. They do really well in school. They might even be very successful. They could be the captain of the basketball team or the drum major in the band. They might get college scholarships! They're very smart and successful, but, unfortunately, they're just not nice people. Nobody likes to be around them. They have this view that they're better, smarter, or more successful than other people. Our goal is to raise children who are smart and successful, but also nice.

Teaching children to be nice isn't complicated. To do so, you only need to know two words. If your children understand these words, and you continually emphasize and stress these two words and ideas to your children, you are going to have children who are not only smart and successful. You're going to have children who are nice and others like to be around.

Edify

The first word they need to understand is edify. Edify is an old word, which comes from the Latin word "aedificare," which means to erect a house. Edify means to build up. In using this word with your children, tell them that edifying (or building up) is their goal in all situations. In any situation, your goal is to build up other people. When you're talking to someone, your goal is to build them up. When you're listening to someone, your goal is to build them up. Regardless if it is your friends at school, your parents, your brothers, your sisters, or your cousins, there is an opportunity to edify in everybody you come in contact with.

Once you have your child thinking about and using this word, the process is very simple. You simply break things down into actions that edify and actions that don't edify. In your conversations, ask, "Did that edify the other person or did that not edify the other person?"

Unfortunately, there are times when we don't edify, or build other people up. When we insult other people, it does the opposite and tears them down. If the only way we can think of ourselves as good or adequate is to tear down other people, that's not going to make a lot of people think we're nice.

Instead, if we approach every conversation and interaction by considering how we can build up the other person, how we can help them feel better about themselves or look better among their peers or family members, we edify them. When I'm writing a letter, filling out a birthday card, giving feedback to someone, answering questions, and even when I'm smiling or not smiling with people at the store, the only question going through my mind is, "How can I edify? How can I build up other people and improve their lives?" When I help other people feel good about themselves, that's edify.

In this chapter, I've included a list of things you can do, or talk to your children about, that will help them understand what edify is and how to edify other people. The goal is for you to be consistent in your explanations. If you use a lot of different words with your children, sometimes using words like nice, polite, friendly or supportive, your children may be confused about what edify really means and what to do in different situations. To avoid that confusion, always come back to the word "edify." Were you edifying or not? Do you think that would edify the other person or not?

The opposite of edify is to tear down. Therefore, naturally, when we tear down other people, insult, try to make ourselves look better, brag, or take credit when it's not ours, we are not edifying anyone but ourselves. If you create this contrast with your children, teach them this concept, and model edification every opportunity you get, there's a high chance that your kids are going to be great edifiers.

Abundance

The second word you need to talk to your children about is abundance. Abundance means plentiful, that there is plenty to go around for everyone. The opposite of abundance is scarcity. Scarcity means there's not enough for everyone, so I have to be out there trying to get my own. I have push other people away so I can get my fair share. People who live their life surrounded by and believing in abundance live a happier life. People who believe in scarcity are always in competition, pushing others aside, and trying to step on other people to raise themselves up and hold others down because they don't believe there is enough to go around.

From the time they are very young until they leave the family home, you can model and practice abundance in every aspect of your child's life. When you put cookies on a tray and your children quickly reach to grab one, trying to beat their friends to the biggest cookie, teach them abundance. "There's plenty of cookies to go around. If we run out of cookies, we'll make more." When you compliment one of your children and another child says, "What about me—didn't I do a good job?" or "Why do you always compliment them; why don't you compliment me?" talk to your children about abundance. When it comes to compliments, quantities are not limited. We're never going to run out of compliments. There's an endless supply that can be replenished at will. You don't have to fight each other or steal compliments from one another—that's abundance.

Too many people live a life of scarcity. They believe they have to push other people down so they can get ahead. "If I let other people get things, there won't be enough for me and I won't get what I want." Not surprisingly, when you do that, nobody wants to spend time with you. We all know people who live a life of scarcity. They believe they have to steal the good things in their life—the compliments, smiles, friends, money, gifts, and promotions—they believe everything has to be stolen from others because there isn't enough to go around.

Instead, if you live a life of abundance, you believe that there's plenty to go around ... or if there isn't, that's okay—we can make more. In almost every situation, you will be nicer and friendlier, you will edify and support others more, you will be a good friend, a good son or daughter, mother or father, and brother or sister. Live a life of abundance.

Here again, it's important to be consistent. Abundance is a word that should be used almost every day in your house. The concept needs to be reinforced so it becomes natural and a way of life.

During the years my children were growing up in my house, they heard the words edify and abundance almost every day. They heard these words consistently, because by using them consistently, I always had a foundation to go back to. When they were doing the right things, I could say, "Great job edifying, great job living a life of abundance;" and when they were struggling and making mistakes, I could say, "Was that edifying? Was that living a life of abundance?" This would give them something to think about, and they quickly learned that these are the two foundations of being nice and the path to healthy relationships with others and becoming somebody others want to spend time with.

I've included in this book a list of things you can do to teach your children a life of edifying and abundance. If you simplify being nice down to two things, edify and abundance, you can avoid tearing other people down and avoid living a life of scarcity. If you teach your children these principles, they will grow up to be not only smart and successful, but also nice.

SECTION 3:
SUCCESSFUL

WHAT DOES IT MEAN TO be successful? Well, successful people accomplish the goals that they have set. Successful people achieve the dreams they have dreamt. It is not complicated. The skills that are necessary to become successful are also not complicated. I like to simplify things. When I work with children, I focus on two specific skills that will help them become successful. Those two skills are setting goals and tracking progress. If you can get your child to be good at these two things, they will have the two skills that are necessary to become successful in their lives.

Setting Goals

Let's start with setting goals. Setting goals is one of the keys to being productive. I know a lot of people who are really busy, but they're not getting anywhere or getting anything done. It's like they're running on a treadmill. The reason they're not making any progress is because they do not have a completely defined goal of where they're headed. Helping your children learn how to set goals, goals that are measurable, achievable, and have a time frame attached to them, is a skill that will serve them well in every academic, work, and life setting for the rest of their lives.

From the earliest age, you should talk to your children about their goals. In our home, we had a goal for potty training, a goal for sleeping through the night, a goal for doing our chores, and a goal for doing our homework. These are goals that are set. In the beginning, of course, you will be setting goals for your children. At some point, though, you want to transfer this over to your children so they become the goal setters on their own.

Modeling goal setting for your kids is the first step. Establish goals in your own life. Talk to your children about these goals, show your children what you're doing to accomplish them, and keep track of your progress toward those goals. Don't do this just once in a while or on occasion. Parents should model goal setting and their progress every day, every week, every month, and every year as their children grow and develop. After your children have seen you setting goals, you can teach them how they can do the same in their life.

Not all goals are equal, however. Any goal you set should be measurable. It should be worded in such a way that you are able to tell whether you've accomplished it or not. For instance, setting a goal to save money is different than setting a goal to save $500. Both goals could be accomplished, but the results could be much different. If your goal is too generic, too vague, and not specific enough, it will be difficult to tell if you've really achieved what you wanted.

Assigning a time frame or a deadline to your goal is also extremely important. You might adjust that time frame as you move toward the goal, but it's still important to have a time frame on your goal. Having time frames and deadlines will help keep you on track and motivate you to make actual progress toward your goal. Without a time frame, your pursuit toward the goal can go into infinity, and you'll find that it's too easy to procrastinate and put off any action toward achieving it.

Choosing goals that are achievable is part of this process, as well. Understanding that a good goal is something that's mostly under your control is an important part of the goal-setting process. I shouldn't have a goal of winning the lottery, because winning the lottery isn't under my control. Now, I can have a goal that's not 100% under my control, but it needs to be something that I at least have influence over, so I can take the action steps necessary to get closer to my goal. The influence I have is something that is under my power.

We've already talked about the importance of teaching your children how to be in control, and sometimes not in control. When it comes to goals, the focus should be on control. The best goals are focused on the areas that you control in your own life. As you practice setting goals with your children, it's important to start with extremely short-term goals. What are we going to do in the next 15 minutes? Can we sit still in the car for 15 minutes? Can we practice piano for the next 30 minutes? Can I walk the dog for the next 45 minutes? In the beginning, the time frame for our goals should be one hour or less. You can slowly expand them to longer increments, such as "What are we going to do today? What are the things I want to accomplish by the end of the day?"

I think the best goals are written goals, because putting them in writing allows you to remember them, and you're less inclined to change them as you progress toward the goal. This will make the reflective process at the end of the goal-setting process more valuable. You can't second guess your goal, you can't misremember your goal, you can't change what you were working toward. It's important to have your goals written down.

There's also another important reason to write down a goal—it builds your commitment to take action and achieve it. The two things I like children to do with their goals are to write them down and share them with another person. This solidifies their commitment to that goal and achieving it. If you're going to set a goal, you have to work hard toward it, and writing it down and sharing a goal with another person will solidify this commitment.

After we've set a goal, we want to take action and work hard toward that goal. At some point during this process, we may recognize that we're not getting closer to our goal. If that happens, we have two choices. We can change our goal or change our approach to the goal. The first step should always be to see if there is another approach to the goal that we can take that would help us achieve it. The second option should be to change your goal or adjust your goal so it is more achievable. At some point, the time frame that you have set for the goal will run out; then it's time to reflect, "Did I accomplish my goal or not? If I did accomplish my goal, was it because it was too easy and not challenging enough? If I did it in less than half the time expected, or if I did it very easily and achieved much more than the goal I had set, perhaps the next time I set a goal, it should be a higher goal or have a shorter time frame."

"If I did not accomplish my goal, was it because the goal was unachievable, and I should adjust the goal?" or my preference, "Can I change my approach to my goal, or simply adjust the time frame for my goal?" These are all great conversations that you should have with your children every day, every week. A great conversation before you go to bed every night is, "How did our goals go today? Did we accomplish them, or did we not?" A great conversation at breakfast is, "What are our goals for the day? What are we going to try to accomplish today, and how are we going to achieve those goals?"

If you do this with your children, the time frame gets longer as they grow older. As your children start to age and get older, you can have weekly goals, monthly goals, and a goal for the school year. As your children become teenagers, you should have a goal for each year. Every year, your big goals for that year should have a theme. That will lead you into discussions about goals for the rest of your life. "What career do you want to achieve in the rest of your life? What major accomplishments do you want to make in your life? What are your schooling options after high school?" These are all conversations that are natural progressions of the goal-setting conversations that you started at the youngest of ages.

As your children go through life, this goal-setting conversation will be one consistent part of their lives. It's only half of the conversation. Remember to reflect on the goal and results afterward. Setting goals and then forgetting them doesn't teach your children anything. You have to set goals, and then later reflect upon those goals to see if you took the right approach, had the right timeframe, or had a realistic goal. Your children will get better, and better, and better at this. You have an opportunity to set weekly goals 52 times each year. You have an opportunity to set daily goals 365 times each year. Is there anything that you practice with your child 300 times that they don't get better at? Being a great goal setter is going to be a skill that will serve your children well in every academic, work, and family setting for the rest of their lives. Start now and continue practicing with your children.

Tracking Progress

The second skill your child needs to become successful is the ability to track progress. The ability to track data over time, or track the progress of anything and watch it develop over time, is a skill that separates successful people from unsuccessful people. Tracking progress over time can be modeled and taught to your children in a variety of different ways. In their youngest ages, we can track their height. In my house, we stood up against a chart on the wall every six months, and my parents would mark how tall we were on that chart. Over time, we can see how tall we were growing. This is tracking progress over time.

We always had a chart in our kitchen that kept track of how many wins our baseball team had. I grew up in Milwaukee, Wisconsin, and our baseball team was the Milwaukee Brewers. Every night, my dad would listen to the Brewers game on the radio, and if they won, he would put a "W" on this chart. Over the course of the summer, I would see the number of W's go up, and up, and up. Unfortunately, during those years, there weren't always as many W's as I wanted on that chart, but it was a great way to track and watch progress develop over time.

I remember my dad asking me if I knew how to read the gas meter outside our house. I played outside in our yard for years, and I'd never even noticed the gas meter. He walked me over to that side of the house and showed me how we could keep track of the amount of natural gas our house was using for heating, cooking, and hot water. He had me look at the gauge on the side of the house and write down the reading. The next day, we walked out there again and wrote down the reading so we could see how much natural gas we have used that day.

I didn't really understand why I was doing this, but he asked me to make a chart of it. Every day, I would go out there and keep track of it; and at the end of every week, I would add up how much energy we used that week. At the end of every month, I would add up how much energy we used that month. Then he started to ask questions like, "Was this week a better week or a worse week for energy use?" "It's really cold outside this week," he would say in the middle of winter, "Are we using more energy than we have in the past?" I started to see patterns develop.

Obviously, more natural gas is used in the winter than in the summer. When all of us were at home, we would use a lot of hot water and a lot of natural gas. When my brother would go away to camp and my sister would be away somewhere for a week or two, we would use less hot water and, therefore, less natural gas. I actually started to track this data over time and learn the patterns that happened regularly. I did a similar thing one of my children. My youngest daughter, Sarah, used to love to help me put salt in our water softener in the basement so our water would taste good.

I would carry 50-pound bags of salt into the basement and pour them into the water softener. One day, it dawned on me that I should have my daughter keep track of how much salt our water softener was actually using. I made a chart with her and had her record how many pounds of salt I poured into the water softener every month. In the beginning, she was writing it down on the chart peacefully. Then, like my father did with me, I started to ask her questions. "Did we use more this month, or less this month? Why do you think we used more in some months than other months? How much are we actually spending on salt for our water softener?" As she grew and aged, and as she collected more data, she had better answers to these questions.

To this day, I can see my daughter tackling problems the way we approached the water softener question. She will gather data, look for other solutions, and look at data over time. She does all of this simply because I had her keep track of how much salt we put in the water softener. When my daughter was about 16 years old, I was putting some salt in the water softener one day, and she yelled from the couch, "Hey, do you want me to keep track of that and write that down, or are you going to put it on the chart?" I had to break it to her that there really was no purpose for recording the salt usage on the chart, other than to teach her the lifelong skill of tracking data over time.

By that point, she'd already acquired that skill. She was keeping track of her practice minutes in band, so she knew how many minutes each week she was practicing her instrument. She was keeping track of her grades in every class, so she knew how many more points she needed to achieve a certain grade. She was keeping track of how much food her pet rabbit was going through, so she could tell if her rabbit was eating a normal amount, or more than normal or less than normal. She also kept track of water consumption for the rabbit, so she could quickly tell if the rabbit wasn't feeling well and consuming less food or water. She had acquired this lifelong skill of tracking data over time.

You can do this. You can do this with your children every day and from the youngest of ages. You can do this with children in whatever area they're interested in. Kids who are interested in sports can track wins on their sports teams. Kids who are interested in math can keep track of the temperature outside or the average number of calories they consume each day. Kids who are interested in music can keep track of how much they practice. Every child can keep track of certain data over time. If you do this with your children, you will raise kids who have a skill that will serve them well in every academic, work, and family setting for the rest of their lives.

When combined, these two skills, setting goals and tracking progress, are the foundations of being successful at work, in school, and in life. If you can teach your child these two skills, practice these skills, and model these skills in front of your children, you are going to raise kids who are not only happy and nice, but are also successful children.

SECTION 4:
SMART

NOW THAT WE HAVE DISCUSSED being happy, being nice, and being successful, it's time to tackle being smart. I use a much broader definition of smart than most people. I don't think all of one's smarts can be identified or measured in a standardized test in school. I don't think they show up in an IQ test. I don't think there's any way with a single test to actually measure how smart you are. I think some people are book smart, while other people are street smart. I think some people are fact smart, while other people are relationship smart. So I use a much broader definition of smart than most people. But regardless of your definition, being smart involves knowing certain things and being able to do certain things. It is a combination of knowledge and skills.

There are specific activities you can do with your children to help give them more knowledge and more skills. If you look at the traditional school subjects of reading, writing, mathematics, social studies, science, and other subjects, you will see that there are specific activities you can do throughout your children's life that will help them perform better in those subject areas. A portion of this book is filled with sets of activities that you can do at any age, at any time, with your children to help them do better in math, reading, and writing.

In addition to these activities, there is no substitute for a simple technique called "think out loud." Think out loud, or what I sometimes call parental monologue, is the concept of not just doing the right thing in front of your children, but talking out loud as you do the right thing. Parents who hold this continual monologue in front of their children as they age and grow are not just showing their children the right thing to do, they're showing them why it's the right thing to do.

From the youngest age, when your kids are in car seats in the car with you, you can talk them through your day. Talk about why you're choosing a certain parking place, why you're waving someone else through a stop sign, why you pulled over on the side of the road when an ambulance went by, why you warmed up your car, and why you locked your car when you walked away from it. When you're at home cooking in the kitchen, you can talk your way through what you're doing and your day. Every decision you made will be explained to your children. This prompts children to think about the why behind certain activities and certain actions. Instead of just knowing what to do, they know why they should do it. Children who have had this why being explained to them from the very beginning don't just make the right decision—they know in any situation why it is the right decision.

As your children grow older and start to understand the conversations you're having and can participate in them, these monologues can turn into dialogue. As you walk your way through your day, you can discuss with your children, "What do you think I should do here? Why would that be the right thing to do?" You can always make sure your children are with you in the decision-making process so they make smart and wise decisions.

It is important that parents understand that there are different types of "smart." While some children may be book smart, others may have more common sense or better relationship skills. This is why I believe that every child is a genius ... just in different ways!

PART 2:

ACTIVITIES

SECTION 1: HAPPY

CONTROL ACTIVITIES

Control Activity #1: Take Turns Choosing the Next Activity

It seems like a simple concept, but allowing your children to take turns in choosing the next activity can help your child practice two very important skills: being in control and not being in control. Whether you're playing games outside or playing board games in the basement, take turns choosing who gets to choose the next game and set a timer for how long you're going to do that activity. This will give your child a chance to practice being in control when it's their turn to choose the next activity, and not being in control when it's not their turn to choose the next activity.

As you go through each of these roles, teach your children that when they choose the next activity, they should choose one everyone likes, and they should pay attention to the needs and wants of the other people participating. And when it's not your turn to choose the next activity, make sure you play along, regardless of your level of enthusiasm for this activity. Be a good follower. Being in control and not being in control requires us to think of others and be a good follower at certain times.

Control Activity #2: Meal Planning

Another way you can teach your children to be both in control and not in control is when it comes to meal planning. On certain nights of the week, the parents will choose the meals. The children then become the followers. They follow along with that meal and accept what is served. On other nights during the week, allow the children to plan the meals. This puts them in control. Once again, you can teach them to be a good leader through the process of thinking of others.

In many households, on Monday, one child gets to pick the meal. On Tuesday, the next child gets to pick the meal. On Wednesday, another child gets to pick the meal, and the parents get to pick the meal for the rest of the week. This way, each child is in control one night a week, but on the other nights of the week, they are being a follower.

Control Activity #3: Vacation Planning, Day by Day

Another way you can help your child practice both being in control and not being in control is in the area of vacation planning. If you're going to take a multi-day vacation, allow each child to plan certain activities on certain days of the vacation. This will put them in two roles. On the times and days that they get to plan the activities, they are in control. Help them to think of others' needs and wants and help them make decisions, even though they might not be popular with everyone. On the other days, when that child is not in control, help them to be a good follower and actively and enthusiastically participate with full effort in the activity, trying to make it as fun as possible.

Vacations are a stressful time for everyone, and practicing the idea of being in control and not being in control is particularly valuable when you have a little less sleep and a little more stress. For that reason, vacation time is a great time to practice these two skills.

Control Activity #4: Identify and Talk about Good Leaders

Part of your role as a parent is to hold a continual dialogue with your children about the things you're seeing and the things you're thinking. As you go through this conversation of life, day by day, make sure you point out and talk about the good leaders you see. That could be a good leader at the grocery store who's leading other workers. It could be a good leader at your church. It could be a good political leader that you see on television, or one of your bosses at work. Good leaders are all over the place, from good coaches to the person who runs your neighborhood association.

What makes a good leader? What makes you like a leader? What makes you want to follow certain leaders?

These are the things you should be talking about with your children. As your children grow older, include them in the conversation. Who do they like to follow? What makes them want to follow that person? What makes a good leader?

Control Activity #5: Identify and Talk about Good Followers

Along with your conversation about good leaders, you should also have conversations with your children about good followers. What makes a good follower? Is it someone who complains the whole time they are following? Is it someone who follows when they want to do the activity, but doesn't follow when they don't want to do the activity? Is it someone who's constantly trying to take over as the leader and take control of every situation? Or on the other hand, is a good follower someone who always enthusiastically participates in the activity, offers advice to the leader, but never tries to take control and encourages others to be good followers, as well?

As you go through your day-to-day life with your children, point out good followers and those times when you're being a good follower, when they're being a good follower, and when others are being good followers. Point out the characteristics that make people good followers, and when you see them, make sure to applaud them. This will help your children not only be good leaders, but also good followers. Not only will it help them be in control, but it will help them in those times when they cannot be in control.

SECTION 1: HAPPY

COMPETENCE ACTIVITIES

Competence Activity #1: Person of the Moment

Person of the Moment is a game you can play almost anywhere. We play it around the kitchen table. When you play person of the moment, one person in the family is chosen as the person of the moment, and everyone else takes a turn saying one thing they like about that person. When it comes back to the person of the moment, that person says something they like about themselves. This is a great self-esteem boosting activity for your children, because they get to hear good things about themselves. More important, it's great practice at saying good things about themselves. If children never learn to compliment themselves and know their strengths and what they're good at, they're never going to have a positive image of themselves and will never going to feel competent in what they do.

As soon as children can talk, they should be old enough to answer these simple questions: What are your strengths? What's something you're really good at? What do other people like about you? Playing person of the moment really helps with this, because not only do your kids get to hear suggestions from other people at the table, they also get to determine the things they like about themselves and share those with others. We play person of the moment on long car rides, when we're waiting for a table at a restaurant, around the kitchen table, just about anytime we have free time. It really helps boost the self-esteem of my children and helps them feel competent about themselves.

Competence Activity #2: Name Your Strengths

The next activity isn't a game or an activity; it's just something that you should do with your children and practice with them. It is called name your strengths. As soon as they are old enough to talk, every child should be able to name the things they're good at. They should have a list of some things that they're working on and some things that they already are pretty good at.

It is the role of the parent to help their child discover these strengths. Sometimes you have to put your children in a lot of different activities, from chess club, to Tae Kwon Do, to soccer, to piano lessons, to find their strengths and the things that make them feel good about themselves. You can also notice and point out characteristics about them on a daily basis, such as being kind, gentle, or patient, to include in their list of individual strengths.

Be sure to look for both interpersonal skills and athletic performance skills. In the end, the goal is that your child has things they can lean on, turn to, and go toward when they're not feeling good about themselves and use them to get back to a place where they feel strong and confident. Again, one of the most important part of this process is that every child has his or her own unique strengths and should be able to identify and name them.

Competence Activity #3: Things I Like

Another activity that it is beneficial to participate in with your children is to have them name things they like. When it comes to decision making time, it is important that children know how to state their preferences without offending other people. For instance, if they are going to a friend's house for dinner, they may be asked what they would like to eat. Being able to name one or two things that you like for dinner, without putting down others and their choices, is an important part of this process.

It shows that you have the confidence to state what you like without downgrading other things. Remember, saying you like something doesn't mean you have to say you don't like other things. If you absolutely hate eating broccoli, instead of saying, "I hate broccoli," you could say, "I prefer carrots," or "I like carrots." When asked, "What you want to do? What do you want to play next?" children should be able to name some games that they like. When asked, "What type of music do you want to listen to, or what songs do you like?" children should be able to say, "This is what I like." Every child should be able to considerately state the things that they like, without being timid or hesitant. This ability to do this shows that they have confidence and belief in themselves, without having to put other things down.

Competence Activity #4: Positive Thoughts Jar

Perhaps you have seen or experienced the power of a jar full of positive thoughts. It has been used in many situations, from a classroom full of students writing positive things on a piece of paper and putting them in an envelope for somebody, to children making a positive thoughts jar for their parents and writing down things they like about their parents. The idea behind a positive thoughts jar is that it is filled with slips of paper, each with a positive thought on it, and each day, or each time you're struggling with your thoughts, you open the jar and pull out a positive thought. I love it when we play person of the moment and we write down some of the compliments for the people in our family and put them in their positive thoughts jar.

Most important, children should be able to write their own positive thoughts down when they're feeling good about themselves and they're having a good day—then they can pull them out and read them on bad days, when they're not feeling good about themselves. Creating a positive thoughts jar or box can be fun. The child decorates the jar with their name and labels it their own positive thoughts jar or jar full of good things. Then give them small slips of paper that they can draw things on or add pictures to. You can help them write down positive thoughts if your children aren't writing yet or don't want to write, and fill the jar with 10, 15, or 20 positive thoughts. If they're having a bad day, they can pull out a positive thought, or they can use it every day, starting their day by reaching into the jar and pulling out a positive thought.

Competence Activity #5: Can We Do It? Yes, We Can

A final activity that you can do to help boost self-confidence and resilience in your children as they view themselves as competent strong people relates to their positive self-talk. It's one thing to be able to say, "I can do it," but research actually shows that it's better to ask yourself a question, "Can I do it?" "Can we do it?" is a question you can ask yourself, "Can I do it?" You should answer the question, "Yes, I can, and here's why," and give reasons why you can do it. "Can I win my basketball game this weekend? Yes, I can." Why? "Because I've been practicing, because I've been playing basketball for a number of years, because I'm not the only one on the team, because we have a good coach."

"Can I do well on the test in school?" "Yes, I can." Why? "Because I've been studying, because I work hard, because I'm going to give my full effort, because I have a good math teacher." There are lots of reasons why. Positive self-talk is great to say, "I can do this."

Remember, it's even more valuable to get your children asking the question, "Can I do it? Yes, I can, here's why."

These are just some of the activities you can do to help raise the competence level and confidence that your children have. Boost their self-esteem and their belief in themselves with these activities.

SECTION 1: HAPPY

RELATIONSHIP ACTIVITIES

Relationship Activity #1: Practice Meeting New People

It is important that you create opportunities to practice introducing yourself to new people, and this teaching should include how to break into an existing group. When you and your child walk up to a new group of people, you should lead by introducing yourself to the new people and then encourage your child to introduce themselves to new people. When you break into a group of adults who are talking, do a little post-teaching afterward and teach your child, "This is how I waited for a time to break in. I waited for everyone else to quit talking, and then I leaned forward and introduced myself or said hello to everyone in order to join the group."

Then you want to create opportunities for your children to meet new people. This could be play dates. This could be introducing them to classes or groups. This could be just going to a public park and walking up to small groups of people or other parents with their children and giving your child an opportunity to introduce themselves to new people. Of course, it's going to be difficult in the beginning. Your child is going to be shy. They're not going to want to hold out their hand or shake hands. They're not going to speak very loudly. This is where your great teaching ability as a parent comes through. You can help them each step of the way by not criticizing them, instead by offering suggestions to help them be more successful the next time they do it.

Relationship Activity #2: Model and Teach Inclusiveness

An important part of the relationship-building process is not to pre-judge people or exclude people, so with your modeling and teaching, I want you to show your children what inclusiveness looks like. Whenever you are in a group of people, keep an eye open for people who aren't part of your group. If you're at a party or a family get-together, look for people who are sitting alone and invite them into your group. If you're sitting in the bleachers watching a sporting event, look for people who are sitting alone and go sit by them and include them in your group.

When you do this, make sure you teach your children about it. Talk to them about it afterward and tell them why you did it (so that no one is alone) and how you did it. Reflect on how easy it is to walk up to someone and say, "Hey, can I sit here? Would you like to join our group?" Those are simple little statements that model and teach inclusiveness. When your children are inclusive with other people, especially those people who are not often included in social groups and social situations, they are going to be great at forming relationships.

Relationship Activity #3: Model and Practice Diversity

Along with inclusiveness, it's important that you model and practice diversity in your relationships with your children. You should look for people who don't look like you, don't act like you, don't live like you, and don't always make decisions like you and include them in your conversations. This doesn't mean you have to become best friends with them. It simply means you should be friendly with them.

When you're at the grocery store, the park, or a sporting event, don't hang around only with people who talk like, act like, and look like you. Reach out and make an effort to include and talk to other people, and then create opportunities for your children to do the same. Introduce and expose them to children who have different backgrounds, different experiences, and different family situations.

By modeling and practicing diversity, your children will become comfortable in all relationship situations, and their available set of friends and relationships will expand with each and every group of diverse people you introduce them to.

Relationship Activity #4: Be Classless

Serve others at all levels. Most people find it easy to form relationships within their same socioeconomic group. An important part of expanding your relationship horizons is to be classless. That doesn't mean to act with no class. It means to ignore classes when looking for other people to serve. It's okay to serve the richest person in your community, and it's okay to serve the poorest person in your community. You might think that some people don't need any help, but they might like a conversation or a kind word. There will be others who you think need a lot of help, and you'd love to serve them in your community.

With my children, we always look to serve others. That could be to help someone return a grocery cart to the grocery store. It might be to hold a door for somebody. It might be to grab an umbrella and help someone get into a building without getting wet. We don't look at who needs extra help because everyone likes to be served and everyone needs a kind word now and then. With a friendly smile, a friendly handshake, a friendly gesture, and by offering a little bit of help, we can show our children that class does not hold them in any category or come with any restrictions. You can serve everyone in this world if you simply reach out and try. People who do this have a wide variety of relationships at many levels.

Relationship Activity #5: Multiple Peer Groups

One of the best things you can do to help your children with their relationships is to engage your child in multiple peer groups. This might include a peer group at school that is different from a peer group in your neighborhood, which is different than a peer group in one of their interest classes, such as a soccer club, Tae Kwon Do class, or a choir. And these are all different than the peer group of their relatives. Having separate peer groups is especially important as your children get older because conflicts will occur. When you are being rejected by students at school, it's great to have some neighborhood friends to turn to.

If you're feeling lonely and nobody wants to play with you in your neighborhood, it's great to have some friends who play basketball or friends in another interest activity. If you feel like you're not getting along with anybody in your Tae Kwon Do class, it's important to be able to have some relatives, cousins, aunts, and uncles you can go to where you have safe, friendly, comfortable relationships.

By putting your child in multiple peer groups, you aren't putting all of your eggs in one basket. You're spreading out the risk of conflict within a relationships, but you're also teaching children that they aren't reliant on a single relationship. Children who are reliant on a single relationship are more likely to give in to peer pressure, to be excluded and worry about being excluded, and to suffer a variety of problems in their relationships than children who have multiple peer groups.

Engage your children in multiple peer groups in different settings that might overlap a little bit but are certainly not completely overlapping, and your children will have lots of options in every situation. These are just some of the activities you can do to improve the relationships that your children form.

SECTION 1: HAPPY

RELEVANCE ACTIVITIES

Relevance Activity #1: Talk about People's Jobs

Remember the goal of building relevance into a child's activities in their daily life is to help them create a plan for the rest of their lives. By exposing your children to different jobs, you help them see the possibilities that exist. Most parents only talk about one or two jobs, which usually consists of the parents' jobs. I want you to go through life in constant conversation with your children, and part of that conversation should be about the jobs that other people have.

Whether you see a bus driver driving a bus, a store manager managing a store, or a salesperson selling carpeting, you should be there to talk about, "What would it be like to do that? Would that be fun to do that? Do you sit behind a desk all day, or do you get to walk and move around? Do you get to spend a lot of time with people? What do you think the bad parts of that job are?" Then connect the job to your child's strengths and weaknesses, the things they like to do, and the interests they have. If you talk more about people's jobs, your child will go through life with an eye open to discover, "What do I want to do for the rest of my life to make money, support my family, and be a productive member of society?"

Relevance Activity #2: Keep a Jobs Book

You should help your child develop a Jobs Book where you record the jobs you have investigated with your child. At the end of every day, before they're getting ready for bed, pull out this little spiral notebook and write down any jobs you noticed that day. Make one page for each of the jobs where you could, over time, fill in the strengths and weaknesses of that job and list other people you know who have that job. If you have an opportunity to interview or talk to someone who has that job, you could take your Jobs Book with you and write down things they tell you about that job. You might even want to arrange a few job shadow activities with your child to give them a chance to experience a day with somebody who has certain jobs.

In the beginning, there might only be one or two jobs in your Job Book. That's okay. As you go through life with your children, you'll point out more and more jobs, and the Jobs Book will fill up. By the time they get to middle school or high school, they'll have lots of jobs to consider.

Parents are in a unique role to match their children with certain jobs. You know your child best. You know their strengths; you know their weaknesses. You know their interests and hobbies. You know what they love, as well as what they don't love. You know about a lot of jobs, especially if you've been filling out a Jobs Book.

You are in a unique role to talk to your children about potential jobs and careers. "With your strengths, this might be a job that you like," or "Because you don't like doing this, I'm not sure that would be a great job for you, unless something changes." It's important that we help our children find jobs that don't feel like work, but instead feel like they're doing something they love to do and are passionate about every single day. Help your child find a job like that, and they'll never have to work a day in their life, but they'll get paid for doing something they love.

Relevance Activity #3: Special Roles

One thing some parents do to help their children find relevance and a plan for the rest of their lives is to assign special roles to each child. Special roles are better than chores, because your child gets to be in control when they have a special role. For instance, if you give your child the chore of putting away the laundry, they're not in control of anything. If you assign them the special role of Laundry Master or Menu Planner, they get to be in charge. Be creative with your roles—a child might be in charge of leaving on time, the entertainment in the car, organizing the house library, or decorating your front door.

You can come up with as many special roles as you want. It's important to assign these special roles to your children because it puts them in control, making it more like having a job than just doing chores.

Relevance Activity #4: Jobs of the Future

As a parent, one of your roles is to help your children learn about jobs of the future, not jobs of the past. We all grew up with a picture of jobs; we knew what our parents did for a living—but we had little or no knowledge of future jobs. We may need to research a little on the Internet, pay attention to some news stories, and read about the industries and types of jobs that are growing and needed in the future. No parent wants to see their child spend years in school, paying for training or a college education, only to find themselves with a degree, a certification, or qualifications for a job that doesn't exist or a job without any available openings.

Instead, we want our children to do something they love and are passionate about, but also a job that is in high demand so they will have flexibility in where, when, and how much they work. Part of that process is learning about jobs of the future.

These are just some of the activities you can do to help your child feel relevant in their life. They will begin to understand that the knowledge they gain does, indeed, have a purpose in their future, and they'll see that there is a bigger purpose for learning than simply being able to complete a classroom assignment or doing household chores.

SECTION 2: NICE

EDIFY ACTIVITIES

Edify Activity #1: Write Thank-you Notes

Writing thank you notes is an important activity you can participate in with your children that will help them learn to edify others. To make sure there is no misunderstanding, I am not referring to thank you texts, thank you emails, or thank you phone calls. This activity involves writing real, handwritten thank you notes that are placed in envelopes, addressed, stamped, and mailed. The process of writing on a piece of paper why they are thankful for someone else is a ritual and an important part of the process. Folding it, putting it in an envelope, addressing it, and putting a stamp on it are not only activities your children will enjoy when they're young and be able to participate in when they're older, but it is a great way to put extra effort in to edify others.

Of course, it's faster to send a text and it's easier to send an email, but part of edification is not taking the easy way out and going the extra mile to help someone else feel edified.

Edify Activity #2: Positive Feedback

Every day, you should set a goal to brighten the day for other people. You can do this in many ways—with a smile, a friendly hello, or by giving positive feedback to a person as you meet, greet, or talk to them. One activity I like to participate in with my children is finding the people whose day we want to brighten and not only give them positive feedback, but also share it with their boss.

If we're at the store and a clerk or someone in the bakery is giving us really good service, we will not only say, "Hey, you're doing a great job; we appreciate you making this a great day for us," but we'll also ask them, "Is your manager around? I'd like to talk to your manager." Then we'll tell their manager the positive feedback, as well.

At the end of every day, as you're getting ready to help your kids go to bed, ask them, "Whose day did you brighten today?" Or you can go around the table and have everybody list, "This is what I did to brighten someone's day today." If you consistently ask each other, "Whose day did you brighten today?" you're going to raise this up as a value in your house, and your kids are going to become great at edifying others.

Edify Activity #3: Talk about Other People

Almost every person in the world talks about other people behind their backs at certain times. This is true whether you leave someone's house and you're talking about what happened at their house, or you leave a sporting event and you talk about what happened at that event. When this happens, you're talking about people and they're not in the room. The problem is so many people do this in a negative way. They gossip, spread rumors, and are critical of other people when they're not in the room.

I want you and your children to get into the habit of talking about other people behind their backs, but in a positive way. When you walk out of a situation, ask, "What was the thing you liked most about that situation?" When you leave a sporting event, say, "Who did you think did best today?" You're doing what comes naturally and talking about other people, but now you're always emphasizing the positive. And if the conversation ever turns critical or negative, swing it back around and say, "Oh, let's not talk about that; let's talk about the positive things. Let's focus on the positive."

Edify Activity #4: One Simple Rule

If you want your children to become great at edifying others, you will teach one simple rule in your household: "Never say something about someone that you would not say in their presence." In other words, if you're saying something about another person, you should only say things that you would say if they were in the room with you. You should only say things about someone that you would say to their face. It's a simple litmus test that any parent can use on anything they say. If you're talking to one of your friends about one of your neighbors, ask yourself, "Would I say this if my neighbor was right here next to me?" If you're talking to one of your cousins about another cousin, would you say that about them if they were in the room? Teach this rule to your children and hold it up as a value that your family never waivers on. Only say things about people that you would say if they were actually in the room—not only is it a simple rule, but it will help your children become great at edifying others.

SECTION 2: NICE

ABUNDANCE ACTIVITIES

Abundance Activity #1: Let Others Go First

Pushing to get to the front of the line is one of the sure signs of scarcity. Remember, abundance is the opposite of scarcity. One of the daily practices we want to instill in our children is letting others go first. When you're waiting in line for a drink of water, and being last in line won't hurt you, let others go first. We're not going to run out of water. Or if you're waiting in line at McDonald's, you don't need to skip other people in line or push to get to the front of the line. McDonald's is not going to run out of food. Letting others go first takes away the fear that we're going to run out of things. It takes away the fear that, "I'm not going to get mine."

Letting others go first serves others, puts others above you, and it teaches abundance. Model going to the back of the line and letting other people go in front of you. At the bank, look for people who appear to be in a hurry and let them get in line in front of you. At the grocery store, look for people who have fewer items in their cart and offer to let them go in front of you. You can let them go before you even if they have more things in their cart than you do. The cash register isn't going to run out of whatever is in a cash register. The store's not going to close; you're still going to be able to buy your groceries.

By letting others go first, you're reinforcing abundance — the idea that there is plenty to go around for everyone — and removing the fear of scarcity in your child's life.

Abundance Activity #2: Donate

When we donate to others, we're recognizing the fact that we have an abundance. Whether we're donating clothes, toys, books, or money, we're recognizing that there's more than enough to go around and that we've been given plenty. One activity we did with our children before buying new clothes was having them go through their closets and select clothes they didn't wear very often or had outgrown to donate to others. The same thing applies to toys—find the toys you don't play with and let's donate them before we buy new toys.

This process teaches children to become aware of the fact that they have plenty, even a surplus, while others don't have enough. It is a great way to help teach your children abundance and a great way to help them serve others.

Abundance Activity #3: Free Fun

Looking for opportunities to have fun for free will teach your children about the abundant opportunity there is for happiness, regardless how much money you have. Some people think money buys happiness, and they teach this to their children. Those children will live their entire life in scarcity because there's never enough money for all the happiness that a person wants. On the other hand, when parents teach their children that the amount of fun and happiness they can have isn't related to the amount of money they have, their children live a life of abundance. One step in this process is teaching your children how to have fun for free, whether that's going for a walk, to a park, or picking up a stick and making up a game using that stick.

Have fun for free ... then talk about it. Talk about what a blast it was to run around in the park today, how much you enjoyed going for a walk, or how fun it was to joke with each other at the grocery store, even though you didn't buy anything. Talk about the fact that you don't have to spend money to have fun. Fun is free! It's an attitude, not a purchase. Fun is just being happy, and it doesn't cost money. Teach this to your children, and they will live a life of abundance. On the other hand, if you teach children that those who have the most money have the most fun and the most happiness, your children will be destined for a life of scarcity.

Abundance Activity #4: Cook for Others

Nothing builds community like breaking bread. One of the nicest things you can do for another person is cook for them. That could be a whole meal, a dessert, or it could just be a plate of cookies. It doesn't cost a lot to bake a loaf of bread or ten cookies for someone, but it certainly brightens their day and puts you in a mood of abundance. You have a lot of food in your house, and you could share a little bit of that food with other people. Of course, you're not going to just donate a can of food to your next-door neighbor—you're actually going to cook. Cooking for them means you put your personal heart, effort, and story into the donation.

Cooking for others teaches your children abundance. Look for those who need a meal, or just brighten someone's day by baking something and dropping it off to them. It doesn't cost a lot of money, but it does share a lot of love, and it will always teach your children the life of abundance.

Abundance Activity #5: Small Gifts, Big Difference

Some people think it's necessary to be rich in order to be generous and give to others. On the contrary, the size of the gift is rarely what matters when you're teaching a life of abundance. Very small gifts, such as paying someone's 50 cent toll or giving a crossing guard a cold bottle of water on a hot day. Both of these cost less than a dollar, but both of them teach a life of abundance and can brighten another person's day. Small gifts make a big difference, and teaching your children that there isn't a connection between the amount of money that you give and how much happiness you can deliver is an important part of teaching them a life of abundance.

The truth is, we won't always be in a situation where we have a lot of extra money, but we will always be in a situation where we have a smile to share, happiness to spread, joy to include others in, and a kind word to say to those in our lives. Happiness has no price. It is absolutely free, and we can share it with others every single day. Small gifts make a big difference.

These are just some of the activities you can do to help your children learn how to edify and live a life of abundance. Put them together, and you will have children who are not only smart and successful, but children who are also nice.

SECTION 3: SUCCESSFUL

GOAL-SETTING ACTIVITIES

Goal-setting Activity #1: Weekly Goals

One activity you can do with your children to help them become great goal setters is to have them make weekly goals. Every Sunday or Monday, you should sit down with your children and ask them what their goals are for the week.

Goals can be something you want to learn in school, do socially, or something you want to do in one of the activities you're involved in. A good goal is observable and measurable. A good goal is somewhat under your control. You don't want your children to set a goal of winning the lottery. That's not under their control. They could have a goal that they influence, but that isn't completely under their control, but the best goals are things that are completely under your control.

A goal of getting an A on your next test isn't completely under your control, because you don't know if the test is going to be hard or easy. A better goal is to study for 15 minutes every night leading up to the test. That's a goal that is completely under your control. Of course, setting the goal is only half the battle—the other part of the process is to check back on your goal. On Fridays or Saturdays, make sure you set some time aside to look back on your weekly goal and ask yourself, "Was it too easy or was it too hard?"

If I accomplished a goal in just one day, maybe it was too easy. If it was too hard, I have two choices. I can change my goal, or I can change my approach to my goal.

It's important to write goals down. Have a goal notebook or a piece of paper to write your goals on. Then, at the end of the week, you will remember what your goal was and can check your progress toward that goal. This is an important part of this process.

I love my weekly goal-setting time with my children. It gives us a chance to talk about what's important in the week to come and what we learned in the week that just passed. Pick a time to set weekly goals with your children, and they will become great goal setters.

Goal-setting Activity #2: Annual Theme

Each year, you could set a theme for the year. For instance, last year, our theme was meeting new people, and in every situation, we tried to meet more new people than we did the year before. We tried to reach out more, shake more hands, make more introductions, and increase the diversity of the people that we know. We tried to meet more people. In the previous year, our annual theme was generosity. We looked for ways to be more generous, with our time, our giving, our smiles, and our love. You could pick an annual theme that would become your family's theme for the year or maybe just for a season, such as the summer.

Remember to reflect back on your annual theme. Setting long-term goals, along with weekly goals, is an important part of helping your children become great goal setters. Reflecting on your progress is a great way to not only track your progress, but also to show your children the impact that goal setting will have on the results they receive in life.

Goal-setting Activity #3: Event Goals

Prior to attending any event, such as a family reunion, concert, sporting event, or a holiday celebration, you should set a goal for that event. That goal might be to not eat too much. That goal might be to meet one new person. That goal might be to say thank you to your host and hostess. Regardless of the event, you're certain to be able to find several goals you can apply to it. Every person in the family should have a goal for the event, regardless if it is the same goal, or each person has their own unique goal.

Whatever your goal is, you should talk about it with your children. My family does this on the car ride to and from events. If we're headed to the theater, a sporting event, or the grocery store, sometimes we have a goal for what's going to happen when we get there, so the ride home is a great time to talk about if we accomplished your goal or not.

Once again, you ask each person in your family, "What was your goal, and did you accomplish your goal?" This process of setting daily, weekly, and annual goals and checking on your progress is going to be an important part of raising kids who are successful.

Goal-setting Activity #4: Reading Goals

One of the most important goals you can set for your children is a reading goal, whether it's how many books they will read, the number of pages they will read, or how much time they will spend reading. Setting reading goals and keeping track of them on a piece of paper is proven to help children become better readers. Reading to your child at a young age and encouraging them to read on a regular basis will also instill a love for books and reading that will benefit them in school and in life.

If you want your child to be great readers who love reading and use books and the knowledge that reading gives them for the rest of their lives, set reading goals. As soon as your children are reading picture books, you should keep track of which books they read and how much they liked them. When your children enter school, you'll keep track of how many minutes they read, how many pages they read, and the titles of the books they read. I would love it if you would start a notebook before they enter school and keep track of every book that your child reads from now until the time they finish their schooling.

In the end, they will look back on this list of books and they will reminisce about the books they've read. Remember their favorites, as well as the books they struggled with. Keeping track of reading goals is an important part of the intellectual development process, and it is a great example of how setting goals and keeping track of those goals will help your children be successful in school and in life.

Goal-setting Activity #5: Reflection Time

One thing that all of our goal-setting activities had in common is a chance to look back at your goal and see if you actually accomplished it. Setting aside time each day to reflect on the goals you've set on the day you just experienced, while it's fresh in your mind, is an important part of this process. You want to make sure to model for your children this reflection time, and at the end of the day, look back on your day and the progress you made toward your goal.

Did I accomplish what I wanted to accomplish? Did I accomplish my goals? Did I move closer to the goals that I have not yet accomplished? These are the type of questions you should ask at the end of each day and should practice with your children. As their day winds down, have a calm, quiet period of reflection about their day and the goals that they've set, including daily goals, event goals, weekly goals, annual theme goals, and reading goals. All of these goals can be looked at during your reflection time. Your children will sleep better if you do this with them because, instead of being in front of a television or playing video games right before bed, they will have some quiet reflection time.

Doing this will help your children sleep better and develop the good habit of investing in a quiet time to reflect, but it will also help them become great goal setters, one of the keys to being successful.

SECTION 3: SUCCESSFUL

PROGRESS-TRACKING ACTIVITIES

Progress-tracking Activity #1: A Daily Record

With each of your children, you should choose one thing to record daily. This might be the outside temperature, what the stock market closed at, or how many wins your baseball team has. The process of keeping track of something every single day is more important than what you track in your daily record.

A daily record will get your children in the habit of writing down facts and figures about a certain aspect of their life. It could be how many hours of sleep they got, what time they woke up each morning, or which clothes they wore each day. Regardless what you keep track of, if you record something every day, over time, it creates a set of data that will grow, and you will be able to do lots of fun things with it, such as looking for patterns, repetition, trends, or finding similarities differences. This data can be turned into an opportunity to create charts or graphs. It can also create opportunities for your children to do experiments to see what would happen if those facts and figures would change.

More important, you will get your children into the habit of keeping track of data over time, which is one of the keys to raising successful children.

Progress-tracking Activity #2: Energy Use

One great example of something your children can record daily or weekly is the amount of energy your home uses, whether you use natural gas to heat your home, electricity to run your appliances, or the water usage in your household. These are great things to keep track of each day or each week. Your house probably has a meter that keeps track of your utility usage, and most of the time, you can read this meter yourself.

Teach your children how to read the meter and how to record how much natural gas, electricity, or water is being used in your house. Keep track of when it goes up and when it goes down and what causes these increases or decreases. Is it the same or each week, or does it vary widely from week to week? Are there seasonal changes between summer, winter, fall, and spring? Are there changes based on how many people are in the house and whether or not you are on vacation? Who knows, as a bonus, you might even learn some ways to conserve water or use less energy in your home. This is a great suggestion you can use when recording daily or weekly with your children, reviewing what you've recorded, and reflecting on it over time.

Progress-tracking Activity #3: Loose Change

Another great example of keeping track of something over time is to have one or all of your children be in charge of accumulating loose change, whether these coins are found on the floor of your car or on the street, taken off your dresser at night, or left behind in vending machines. Accumulating change is a great way to track data over time because this number will continually go up if they continue to gather change. Your children will be able to measure their progress, while they learn about money and savings.

Each day, they can record how much change they gathered that day and then determine the total amount they've gathered over time. If they do this repeatedly over time, two things will happen. Your children will become great at tracking data over time. They will also learn how real savings happen. Real savings doesn't happen with $1,000,000 deposit into an account. Real savings happens over time, with small deposits made again and again and again. If your children continually put small amounts of change into a box and record how much change they're putting into that box and keeping track of the total, they'll see this is how money grows—not with one big deposit, but with small deposits made consistently and over a period of time.

Accumulate and gather change with your children, record the change that they gather, and then record the total, and you will teach your children two valuable lessons: tracking progress over time and how money is actually saved.

Progress-tracking Activity #4: Saving Toward a Goal

Allowing your children to choose something they would really like, whether it's on a website or out of a catalogue, determining the price of that item, and then saving money toward that purchase is a great activity you should participate in with your children. It teaches them two important concepts: tracking money saved over time and saving for something before they buy it, rather than buying it before they have enough money.

Here's an activity you should do: Allow your children to pick an item that they really want, but don't have enough money to purchase right now. Then allow them to save money over time, setting that money aside in an envelope for that specific purchase. On the front of the envelope, write the name of the item you're saving for and how much money is in the envelope. Every time you add money to the envelope, record the deposit and recalculate the total.

This is how successful people buy things. They save money and when they have enough money, they buy what they want. If you can teach your child these two valuable lessons, tracking the progress of their savings over time and saving money for something and delaying the gratification until they have enough money to buy it, you will set them up for a life of success and sound money management for the rest of their lives.

Progress-tracking Activity #5: Exercise

Another example of something your children can track easily each day and over time is how much exercise they get. Whether this is the number of steps they take each day or the number of minutes that they exercise, walk, or run each day, keeping track of this over time will have two important by-products. The first is you will teach your children how to track data over time. Each day, they can record the number of steps they take on their pedometer and then total it at the end of the week and the end of the month. They can see if it is the same every week and every month, or if it changes from week to week and/or month to month. If there are increases or decreases, start a discussion with your child about why that happened. Are there seasonal changes? Is your activity level different in winter than it is in summer?

In addition to the valuable lesson children gain from tracking data over time, they get a bonus by-product and can see that exercise is a daily and weekly activity, not just something they do once a year or only at special events. Spreading your exercise out over time and making it a daily part of your life is the healthy choice for them to make. As a result, they will see how small amounts of exercise each day add up and benefit them, rather than one large burst of exercise each month. Daily and consistent exercise is a healthier, more stable way to maintain fitness and an active, healthy lifestyle.

Tracking your own exercise over time is a great way to teach these two skills and great way to teach by example the importance of a healthy lifestyle filled with daily exercise.

Progress-tracking Activity #6: Recording Practice

Another way to help your child learn how to track progress is to keep track of the amount of time that they spend practicing a certain activity. Counting the actual number of minutes they practice a certain activity shows them how hard work pays off with real results.

If your child is learning how to play piano, have them keep a chart of how many minutes they practice piano. If your child loves to play basketball, have them keep a chart of how many minutes they play basketball or practice shooting hoops. If your child loves to cook, have them keep track of how many minutes they actually spend in the kitchen preparing dishes and cooking.

The end result of this is twofold. First, your child will learn how practice builds up over time. Instead of practicing for four hours one day, they can see that they can practice for one hour each day for a week and end up with seven hours of practice. In the end, when they improve and become good at this activity, you can point to the chart and say, "This is why you are good at something." They'll be able to appreciate their hard work and know that they improved, not because they are lucky or gifted, but because they put in the time, effort, and hard work. Hard work pays off with real results.

You can also point to the chart in the event they don't get the results they wanted or are not as good at something as they wanted to be. Show them that they have two choices: to increase the number of minutes they practice this and get better, or to practice for the same number of minutes, or less, and stay at their current level of ability.

There is a direct connection between the amount of time that you practice and your abilities in many, many things. You can attach these two things together by tracking and keeping a record of practice time with your children. Keeping track of practice over time is great for two reasons. It helps your children learn how to attract progress, and it shows them that hard work pays off with real results.

These are just some of the activities you can do to help your children become great goal setters and progress trackers. You can do some or all of them, or make your own activities, to help your children set and accomplish their goals throughout life.

Remember, there are two skills every child needs to be successful. The ability to set goals and reflect back on those goals, and the ability to track their progress over time. Ideally, your house would be filled with little charts, lists, and graphs reflecting your children and their goals and the tracking of their progress over time. These records are a sign of a house that will be filled with a successful children.

SECTION 4: SMART

READING ACTIVITIES

Reading Activity #1: What's the Perfect Word?

When you play this activity, show your child a picture and ask, "What's the perfect word to describe this situation?" Allow your child to brainstorm different words to describe the picture. "There's always a better word" is a motto in our family. So take multiple suggestions for each picture and play it as a game where you go back and forth, each trying to come up with the more descriptive word that will better describe the situation. You can use pictures from one of your scrapbooks, photo albums, the Internet, newspapers, and magazines. Any picture you find is appropriate when playing the game "What's the perfect word?" Doing so will increase your child's vocabulary and help them understand why certain words are chosen for certain situations.

Reading Activity #2: Shades of Meaning

Shades of Meaning uses three similar words that are close to each other in meaning, but not exactly the same. Have your child draw three different pictures of the words. For instance, you might choose the words angry, furious, and mad, and have your child draw a picture of angry, a separate picture of furious, and a separate picture of mad. Then ask questions. What's different about the pictures? What separates furious from angry? What separates angry from mad? Doing this will help your child discern between words that are close in meaning and help them understand that certain words have different shaded meanings. If you have trouble coming up with sets of words that have similar meanings, just Google shades of meaning, and you will get list after list of words at different grade levels that are appropriate to use when playing this game with your child.

Reading Activity #3: Ping Pong Attitudes

In Ping Pong Attitudes, you write 10 different moods or attitudes on 10 ping pong balls. On one ping pong ball, you might write, "Sad." On another ping pong ball, you might write, "Happy." On another one, you might write, "Worried." Then, put the ping pong balls in a bag. Write down a sentence that both you and your child can read. A typical sentence might be, "I would like some more soup. Please?" Then have your child draw a ping pong ball out of the bag. They look at the word, without letting you see it, and they read the sentence in that tone or mood. If the word is angry, they should sound angry when they read the sentence. If the word is sad, their mood or attitude should be sad when they read the sentence. Based on the way they read the sentence, you have to guess the mood or attitude that was written on the ping pong ball. Being able to discern the author's tone, mood, or attitude in a reading passage is one of the key skills that separates great readers from students who struggle in reading, and the game ping pong attitude will help your child learn this important skill.

Reading Activity #4: Charades

Many families play Charades with silly words or silly phrases. I would like you to play the same game, Charades, with sentences that could be main ideas in a paragraph or story. If you have trouble coming up with these sentences, think of the moral of the story in any story you read. After reading a children's book, a novel, or an article in the newspaper, say, "The moral of the story is ... " and write down a sentence. Put these sentences on slips of paper. Allow your child to draw one slip of paper and try to act it out without saying any words. This game of charades, from the guessing point of view and from the acting point of view, helps your child identify and develop a main idea and how it would be communicated. It will improve both their reading and their writing.

Reading Activity #5: Who's Like This?

To play the game "Who's Like This," get slips of paper and write down words that would describe people, such as happy, greedy, tall, bully, etc. Each player draws a slip of paper from the many slips of paper, and you brainstorm with your child how many people you can name who are like that. This will help them understand different character personalities and motivations, which is an important part of the comprehension process when you're reading a passage. Many families play this as a group game, working together to brainstorm a list. Some families play it as a competition, where each person brainstorms as many people as possible, and whoever has the longest list that meets the approval of everyone else in the family is the winner.

Reading Activity #6: Describe this Person

To play Describe this Person, show your child a picture of a person who they would recognize. If your child is young and reading storybooks, this could be a fictional character. It could be a famous person if your child is in middle school or high school. Then, ask them what word describes this person. That's the first part of the game. But the second part of the game is the important part. In the second part, you ask them why they would describe the person with that word. What is their evidence for describing the person that way? You want them to reach back into the story and what they know about this person and give real reasons. Being able to defend their views and opinions with facts will not only make your child a good reader, it will also make them a great writer, which is why I always play Describe this Person with my children.

Reading Activity #7: Multiple Meanings

In this game, you show your child a word that has multiple meanings. If you don't know words like this, you can Google "words with multiple meanings," and you will get list after list of words with multiple meanings. There are a number of ways you can play this game. I like to play a game of Charades, where the child acts out one of the meanings for the word, and after they've done that, you have them play Charades again and act out a different meaning for the word. This will help your child recognize that different words have different meanings. You can make a list of the words you've learned that have multiple meanings. We keep our list on the refrigerator. We know some words that have two meanings and fewer words that have three meanings. We even know some words that have four and five meanings. By doing this, you'll be tracking data over time with your kids, making a nice long list, while you're playing The Multiple Meaning game.

Reading Activity #8: Out of Order

In this game, you take a sentence and mix up the words so they are out of order. You can do this by typing it on your computer, printing it out, and cutting it up with a scissors. You could also write different words on separate index cards and then mix them up until they are out of order. Your child then tries to put the words in the correct order. This is a great activity to help children improve their early reading skills by putting a sentence back in the correct order. Sometimes I even like to stretch a clothesline across my living room and hang the words on the clothesline with clothespins. My kids love to rearrange the words on the clothesline as they try to make a sentence that makes sense. This is a great activity to help your children realize the natural order of a sentence and help them learn how to arrange words in a sentence so they make sense. Once your children get a little older, they can play the game by writing down a sentence, cutting it into separate words, and mixing up the order, then giving it to you to see if you can put the sentence back in the correct order.

Reading Activity #9: Two Pictures

To play this game, you find two pictures from anywhere—the Internet, a magazine, a book, or a newspaper. Show your child the two pictures for 10 seconds each and then ask them questions. What do these two pictures have in common? What's different about these two pictures? What are some things that are not found in either picture? What is something that's found in the first picture, but not the second picture? This is a great activity to help students develop and access their working memory. Showing the two pictures separately and then taking them away when asking the questions will help your child recall facts and be able to compare and contrast two things that they've been looking at.

Reading Activity #10: READ!

Although it would seem that none of these activities actually involve reading, all of these activities will help your children become better readers. The great part is you can start playing these games with your kids even before they know how to read. Of course, you want to supplement all of these activities with lots of time spent practicing reading, reading to your children, reading with your children, and reading next to your children. Make sure you keep track of all of those minutes, tracking data and progress over time.

SECTION 4: SMART

MATH ACTIVITIES

Math Activity #1: What's the Question?

In this activity, you show your child a picture, and instead of asking a math question from the picture, you turn it around and ask your child, "What math questions could we ask about this picture?" Instead of looking only for the right answer, your child now actually has to think about the math involved in any picture.

If you show your child a picture of a car, instead of asking an obvious math question like, "How long is the car?" ask your child, "Which math questions could we ask about this picture? Which math questions does this picture make you think of?" Your child can start to brainstorm different questions. How much does the car weigh? How long is the car? How tall is the car? How fast does the car go? How many people would fit in the car? These are all examples of great brainstorming questions. Playing this game will help your child think of math not only as something with right or wrong answers, but also as something that is creative and fun. It will greatly improve the way they tackle math problems for the rest of their lives.

Math Activity #2: Transformation Station

Transformation Station is a game where you allow children to move things from pictures into math notation and math notation into pictures. For instance, you could start with the math problem 3+2, and ask your child to draw a picture representing that math problem. For example, your child might draw a picture of three red apples and two green apples. You could also draw your child a picture of 10 apples, then cross three of those apples off, and ask them to write a math problem representing that (10-3=7).

As you go through life, you can transform this activity from pictures to real life. Whenever you encounter something that you could use math for, like "There are six people sitting at a table. How many people should we put on each side of the table?" That's a great math problem to ask your child, and you should recognize it as a math problem and talk to them about it. Can you transform it into a math sentence? Can you draw a picture that represents it and solves it?

Throughout your child's life, as they do mathematics, they are going to have to transform text to math notation, math notation into text, pictures into text, and text into pictures, pictures into math notation, and math notation into pictures. You can practice this from the earliest ages with your children, and they will become great at transformation.

Math Activity #3: Which is Bigger?

Comparing two numbers or two quantities to each other is an important skill that will serve your child well in every math setting they approach or encounter. As you go through your day, you should always be showing your child two different quantities and asking them, "Which is bigger? Which is smaller?" This could be two different lengths, two different volumes, two different weights, two different perimeters, or two different heights. It's a study of comparisons and contrasts, determining which is larger, smaller, longer, taller, heavier, etc. This is a great game you can play from the moment they wake up until the moment they go to bed, and you can do it anywhere—in the kitchen, in the living room, at the store, or in the park. It develops a math skill in your children that they will use again and again.

Math Activity #4: Flexible Number Line

This activity requires you to take a clothesline and hang it somewhere in your house, such as between two chairs or across a wall. You'll also need index cards and a marker. Starting with the numbers 1 through 10, write a number on the index cards and have your child place them in order on the clothesline. Then, you can change the order of the numbers on the line, moving them to the beginning or the end, and talk about the numbers in between. You can use the flexible number line to teach place values, fractions, decimals, and percentages. You can use it to teach ratios. You can guess where 2.5 would be if you have the numbers two and three on the line, and the beauty of it is that you can spread out numbers further and further apart to create more and more space in between them, so your guesses can become more and more accurate.

I've used the flexible clothesline to explain many concepts to my children, and we've used it to play so many games together. Once you hang the clothesline and make your numbered index cards, game after game after game will pop up into your head, from trying to guess what number the other person is thinking of, to estimating how many numbers are greater than a certain number or less than a certain number. The flexible clothesline makes math fun. There are lots of games you can play using your flexible number line. You are limited only by your imagination.

Math Activity #5: Full-sized Graphing

This activity extends the above flexible number line activity into a different direction, forming a two-coordinate graphing system. Picture a giant two-coordinate graph on a wall in your house! You can also do this on the floor, instead of a wall, if you wish. Objects on the wall can become the points as your children try to guess the coordinates of them in an ordered pair. The horizontal axis, or the axis that goes left to right, is always stated first. Zero is on the left, and the numbers go up as you go to the right. The vertical axis goes from zero at the bottom up the left-hand side of the wall or the floor.

Then, every item gets a point. You name the horizontal number first and the vertical number second to give the location of any point. This is a great introduction into two-coordinate graphing for your children. Children who are spatial thinkers will quickly catch on, and this will become one of their real strengths. Some children will see the logic of the graph on the floor easier, since it will look like it does on a piece of paper. Others will see it on a wall better, as it is vertical and horizontal.

Full-size graphing is a fun game that can be expanded outside into your yard, a park, or a field. You can try to guess the positions of certain trees and objects in your yard based on a two-coordinate graphing system.

Math Activity #6: Working Memory

Working Memory is the ability to remember three, four, five, or six items for less than ten minutes. There are many games you can play to practice your working memory, but the easiest is to show your child three, four, five, or six items for a few minutes, and then take them away. Wait one or two minutes, and then ask your child to recall the items. You might start with showing them three numbers for 60 seconds. Take them away for a minute or two, and ask them to repeat those three numbers. Then, work your way up to four numbers, five numbers, and six numbers. You can do this with pictures, objects in your house, numbers, names, letters, or words. There are many different ways you can practice working memory.

Working Memory is a huge separator once your children start to do schoolwork and perform on assessments. Almost every item on every assessment your child will take in any school setting will ask them to store and remember a small number of items. Being able to do so will increase their speed and accuracy, and it will allow your child to show everything they know on any assessment. If your child is one of those students whose test results don't fully reflect their knowledge, it might be because they need some working memory practice. The good news is that all of the research shows that you can increase your working memory with practice. Our working memory strengthens like a muscle, so be sure to play lots of games where you practice working memory.

By the way, if you've ever played the game Concentration, where cards are spread face down on a table and flipped over to try to find a matching pair, you played a classic working memory game. You can replicate this game in your own home with a deck of cards or pictures you and your children draw. It's a great way to practice working memory with your child.

Math Activity #7: Always, Sometimes, Never

Students need practice thinking about different situations that might occur in math and in life. Playing this activity will help them think of the logic between always, sometimes, and never. In this activity, I come up with three different hand motions. For always, I clap my hands above my head. It looks like the letter A. For sometimes, I extend my arms out to the side and rock back and forth like a teeter-totter. For never, I put my arms down at my side. By following the line of my arms over my shoulders, it makes an N, like never. Then, make up sentences for your child and ask them to respond with always, sometimes, or never. Bicycles have two wheels. Always, sometimes, or never? The moon is out at night. Always, sometimes, or never? Happy people smile. Always, sometimes, or never? This is a great kinesthetic game that your children will love to play because they get to bounce around, move their arms, and guess. Get a large group of kids playing it together, and they'll have fun comparing each other's answers and seeing who was right and who was wrong. Everybody loves the game always, sometimes, and never.

Math Activity #8: Technology Websites

It is important that your children understand and can use technology to their best advantage. This will allow them to show everything they know in school, and it will enable them to access the whole world that is available to them on computers and the Internet. There are four essential skills that you should work on with your children. Mouse skills include the ability to move a mouse around a screen and select, drag, and drop certain items.

Navigation skills allow them to see the different parts of a website or in a document on a computer screen. Drag and drop is the ability to move an object from one location to another location. Keyboarding is the ability to enter information using the keyboard of your computer. I have included here a list of websites that provide great opportunities for you to practice these four skills with your children.

MOUSE SKILL WEBSITES:

Starfall Pattern Maze allows students to practice using the mouse while they practice identifying shapes.

http://more2.starfall.com/m/math/geometry-content/play.htm?f&n=geo-maze&y=1&d=demo

Birthday Candle Counting gives students the opportunity to practice using the mouse while they practice one-to-one counting.

http://www.abcya.com/kindergarten_counting.htm

Color, Draw, & Paint gives students the opportunity to draw lines and circles and navigate buttons with their mouse.

http://www.abcya.com/abcya_paint.htm

Balloon Pop Subtraction allows students the opportunity to practice subtraction while practicing their mouse skills.

http://www.abcya.com/subtraction_game.htm

Math Mavens: Students can practice multiple mouse skills, including scrolling, using drop down menus, radio buttons, and accessing links to build their navigation skills.

http://teacher.scholastic.com/maven/index.htm

Mouse Practice Bubble Activity: Students can practice multiple mouse skills, including scrolling, using drop down menus, radio buttons, and accessing links to build their navigation skills.

http://www.letsgolearn.com/bubble.html

Spelling Bees: Students can practice multiple mouse skills, including scrolling, using drop down menus, radio buttons, and accessing links to build their navigation skills.

http://www.abcya.com/spelling_practice.htm

NAVIGATION SKILL WEBSITES:

Word Machine allows students to practice their short vowel sounds, while learning how to look for 'Hot Spots' when navigating websites.

http://more2.starfall.com/m/word-machines/short-a/load.htm?f&d=demo&n=main&y=1

Marvin Makes Music is a read aloud that allows students to practice navigation, while listening to reading.

http://www.abcya.com/marvin_makes_music.htm

In the **Number Chart Game,** students will place numbers in the appropriate location on the number chart while choosing between levels and finding hot spots.

http://www.abcya.com/one_hundred_number_chart_game.htm

Dinosaurs Read Aloud is a read aloud that allows students to practice navigation, while listening to reading. Use hot spots (pause, arrow) and volume sliders.

http://more2.starfall.com/m/talking-library/dinosaurs/load.htm?f&d=demo&filter=first

In Study Jams, students can watch videos and play supplemental games on a variety of topics tied to CCSS

Math standards. Play a video, use navigation tools, and learn!

http://studyjams.scholastic.com/studyjams/index.htm

In Math Word Problems, have students choose a grade level, and practice typing in a constructed response box.

http://www.mathplayground.com/wpdatabase/wpindex .html

Comic Strip: Students will learn to navigate a webpage by reading instructions, clicking items, dragging items, viewing videos, and entering text into fields.

http://www.makebeliefscomix.com/

Friendly Letter: Students will learn to navigate a webpage by reading instructions, clicking items, dragging items, viewing videos, and entering text into fields.

http://www.abcya.com/friendly_letter_maker.htm

Word Clouds: Students will learn to navigate a webpage by reading instructions, clicking items, dragging items, viewing videos, and entering text into fields.

http://www.abcya.com/word_clouds.htm

DRAG AND DROP SKILL WEBSITES:

Starfall 2D & 3D Shapes will allow students to identify 2D & 3D shapes while they practice how to "drag and drop."

http://more2.starfall.com/m/math/geometry-content/load.htm?f&d=demo&n=enviro-shapes&y=1

Zac and the Hat allows students to practice short vowel sounds while they practice how to "drag and drop."

http://more2.starfall.com/m/decodable/zac-hat/load.htm?f&d=demo

In Base Ten Fun, students will practice their "drag and drop" skills by constructing numbers using base ten blocks.

http://www.abcya.com/base_ten_fun.htm

Practice spelling site words by dragging and dropping letters to spell the word.

http://www.abcya.com/dolch_sight_word_spelling.htm

In Math Journey, students will practice their "drag and drop" skills by choosing which numbers are greater or less than by traveling through the journey.

http://more2.starfall.com/m/math/math-journey/load.htm?f&d=demo&filter=first

Thinking Blocks: Students will practice following instructions by dragging and dropping items, thus reinforcing the skills of dragging and dropping within a field.

http://www.mathplayground.com/thinkingblocks.html

Clean-Up Your Grammar: Students will practice following instructions by dragging and dropping items, thus reinforcing the skills of dragging and dropping within a field.

http://www.missmaggie.org/scholastic/cleanup_eng_launcher.html

KEYBOARDING SKILLS WEBSITES:

Monkey Paws: Students will type keys using left and right hands.

http://annrymer.com/keyseeker/

Keyboarding Zoo: Students will practice finding the keys on the keyboard.

http://www.abcya.com/keyboarding_practice.htm

Keyboard Climber: Students will navigate the website to begin and type keys that appear.

http://www.tvokids.com/games/keyboardclimber

Practice keyboarding skills with **Keyboard Invasion.**

http://www.abcya.com/keyboard_invasion.htm

Practice keyboarding skills with **Sky Chase.**

http://www.arcademicskillbuilders.com/games/sky-chase/sky-chase.html

Practice keyboarding skills with **Dance Mat Typing.**

http://www.bbc.co.uk/guides/z3c6tfr

SECTION 4: SMART

WRITING ACTIVITIES

Writing Activity #1: What's in the Bag?

In this game, you put four items into a brown paper bag and show them to your child. Pull out the items one at a time. The object is for your child to say which order the items should be used in, what the four items have in common, and name one more item that could be added to the bag that would make sense.

For instance, you might walk into the room with a brown paper bag and start pulling things out. The first thing in the bag is a rubber spatula. The next item is a bowl. The next item is an egg. The next item is a cupcake tin. Your child might guess that you're going to make cupcakes, which is the correct main idea. The next thing they should do is tell you what order you would use those items in. Finally, they should add one more item to the bag that would make sense, such as a beater or any item that fits the theme of making cupcakes.

Play this game each day with your children. After you've played it a few times, your children can put bags together and play the game with each other. This is a great activity that will help your children learn how to put parts of a story together in order, and how to add to an existing story so they can expand their writing.

Writing Activity #2: Clothesline Mix Up

This activity is also a sequencing activity. You put a series of events on a clothesline that you've hung up in a room or along a wall. Intentionally put the events in the wrong order. Your child then tries to put them in the correct order. Another way to play this game is to cut out a comic strip from the newspaper or the Internet, and place them so the frames are not in the correct order. Your child tries to put the frames of the comic strip in the correct order.

Using a set of index cards, you can also have your child draw a series of pictures that occur in a certain order, and you have to put the items or the events in the correct order. All of these mix-up sequencing games practice telling a story in a narrative sequence. This is an important part of the writing process that many children struggle with. Practicing these activities with your children will help them become better writers.

Writing Activity #3: Double-up Description

Perhaps you've played the campfire game where you say, "I'm going on a trip, and I'm taking a ... " and then you name an object. The next player has to say, "I'm going on a trip, and I'm taking ... " and they name your object and add an object of their own. Each person has to repeat all of the previous answers and add one more to the list. Double-up description is similar to the campfire game, but it uses descriptive words. Choose something that you and your child would like to describe, perhaps a scene out the window or something you're looking at on television or the computer. You say one word that describes it, and the next person has to say your word, plus the next word that describes it. The next person has to say your word and the next word, and then add a word to the list. Go back and forth until somebody cannot remember all of the descriptions for that object. It's a great activity because it practices working memory, an essential skill that your children will need as they go throughout the life, but it also increases the number of words in their vocabulary to describe things.

In the beginning, many children struggle with this game because their description vocabularies are not very good. The more you play this game, the better your children will become at describing things. Your goal to make them great writers is to help them come up with a wide variety of words that can describe different situations. Double-up Descriptions does just that.

Writing Activity #4: Narration Station

In this game, you and your child are pretend announcers in a play-by-play booth, while you're watching a common activity take place. Perhaps you're watching someone walk down the street, and you take turns describing the action like it was the most exciting sporting event ever to happen. Perhaps you're watching someone in your house turn on the television, do the laundry, or cook dinner, and you act as announcers, adding sports-like drama to everyday activities, such as washing dishes, making the bed, or vacuuming the floor. Whatever the activity, announce it like you're in a play-by-play booth and it's the final minute of the biggest and most exciting football game in history.

This gives you a chance to add drama and excitement to everyday language. It will help your child get practice using verbs and adjectives together in the same sentences. One of the hallmarks of an advanced writer is the ability to use verbs and adjectives together, rather than in separate sentences. Narration station helps them practice this specific skill.

Writing Activity #5: Show and Don't Tell

In our house, we play a board game called Taboo, where we are asked to convey the meaning of a word without using any of the words from a list. Of course, if you're being asked to describe a word like horseracing, you can't say the word horse or race, as well as other words on the list, such as Kentucky Derby, to describe that word.

Show and Don't Tell is a similar activity where your children try to convey the meaning of a short sentence without using any words from that short sentence. Your children will have to show you what it means, rather than tell you what it means. This activity, like most of the activities listed here, is an oral game, not a writing game, but the skill they are using is a skill that will help them become better writers. Great writers don't tell you exactly what's happening; they show you through the actions of the characters and the words they use. Eventually, you could practice writing things out like this, but the game will be a lot of more fun and the skill will be passed much more quickly if you play the game orally at first.

Writing Activity #6: Musical Shares

This activity helps move your children from concrete to abstract writing. You give your child a simple action to do, then you play music in the background. Your child has to describe their feelings while doing the action. Their feelings should match the music. Remember, the activity itself, whether it's jumping rope, walking down the street, or climbing a ladder, doesn't always determine the emotion or the feeling. Someone could be mopping the floor cheerfully or with anger. Your child should describe the feeling, then, using the skills developed in activity five, show you the feeling, rather than tell you the feeling.

The background music is optional in this activity, but children really like hearing music behind the actions. When they get old enough to choose their own music from your computer's music library, they will be able to add background music and put a soundtrack behind the actions in this game.

All of these activities will help your children develop and become better writers. The first activities help them categorize and sequence. Then there are some narration activities and description activities. The final activity helps them move from concrete to abstract. Remember, these activities are just suggested frameworks for you to think about when teaching your children the essential skills necessary for reading, writing, and mathematics. You can adjust the activities. You can play them as games. You can teach them as lessons. I like to just build them into the daily conversation that is life in my house. If you do that, they won't feel like school lessons or work. They'll feel like everyday life, where we work on becoming better describers, better mathematicians, and better people who are able to discern the meaning of words.

FINAL THOUGHTS

IN THIS BOOK, WE HAVE discussed how to help your children grow up to be smart, successful, nice, and happy. Some parents achieve just one of these with their children; others achieve two or three. I hope this book has helped show you that there is a path to achieving all four of these with your children. Parenting is not an event. It's not one conversation or one day that makes all of the difference. Parenting is a series of small experiences, small conversations, and small things that your children see you do that have a combined effect on the outcome. There are no guarantees. You can do everything right, and your children can still end up in a place where you don't want them to be, but if you follow the steps in this book, you will have the very best chance of your children becoming smart, successful, nice and happy.

With that as our definition, I believe that every child can be a genius. Your child, my child, every child is a genius. Thank you for taking the time to read this book and putting forth the effort to help your children be successful in school and in life. I would love to hear about your experiences, including what has worked for you and what has not worked for you. Email me any time at pat@parentinggenius.com. I'd love to hear your stories and share your wisdom with others.

62177529R00068

Made in the USA
Lexington, KY
31 March 2017